@RosenTeenTalk
Life Skills

GETTING A JOB IRL

Kathleen A. Klatte

ROSEN
PUBLISHING

Published in 2025 by The Rosen Publishing Group, Inc.
2544 Clinton Street, Buffalo, NY 14224

First Edition

Editor: Greg Roza
Designer: Rachel Rising

Photo Credits: Cover, p. 1 Daniel M Ernst/Shutterstock.com; Cover, Cosmic_Design/Shutterstock.com; Cover, pp. 1, 3–48 Vitya_M/Shutterstock.com; pp. 3, 5 Elena_Alex_Ferns/Shutterstock.com; p. 6 YummyBuum/Shutterstock.com; p. 7 Worawee Meepian/Shutterstock.com; p. 8 smx12/Shutterstock.com; pp. 9, 16 Gorodenkoff/Shutterstock.com; p. 10 Just dance/Shutterstock.com; p. 11 Sharkshock/Shutterstock.com; pp. 3, 12 BearFotos/Shutterstock.com; p. 13 frantic00/Shutterstock.com; p. 14 Creativa Images/Shutterstock.com; p. 15 Krakenimages.com/Shutterstock.com; p. 17 Dmitry Demidovich/Shutterstock.com; pp. 3, 19 Drazen Zigic/Shutterstock.com; p. 20 Irina Strelnikova/Shutterstock.com; p. 21 oliveromg/Shutterstock.com; p. 22 picoStudio/Shutterstock.com; p. 23 Mangostar/Shutterstock.com; p. 24 Pormezz/Shutterstock.com; p. 25 Ground Picture/Shutterstock.com; p. 26 Antonov Maxim/Shutterstock.com; p. 27 Daniel M Ernst/Shutterstock.com; p. 28 fizkes/Shutterstock.com; p. 29 Dean Drobot/Shutterstock.com; p. 31 KOTOIMAGES/Shutterstock.com; p. 32 Lisa F. Young/Shutterstock.com; pp. 3, 33 Harismoyo/Shutterstock.com; p. 34 Andrey_Popov/Shutterstock.com; p. 35 Lisa-S/Shutterstock.com; p. 36 Viktoria Kurpas/Shutterstock.com; p. 37 SFIO CRACHO/Shutterstock.com; p. 38 rnl/Shutterstock.com; pp. 3, 39 Andriy Blokhin/Shutterstock.com; p. 40 Ariya J/Shutterstock.com; p. 41 Perfect Wave/Shutterstock.com; p. 43 Rawpixel.com/Shutterstock.com; p. 45 Dragon Images/Shutterstock.com.

Some of the images in this book illustrate individuals who are models. The depictions do not imply actual situations or events.

Library of Congress Cataloging-in-Publication Data

Names: Klatte, Kathleen A., author.
Title: Getting a job IRL / Kathleen A. Klatte.
Other titles: Getting a job in real life
Description: [Buffalo] : Rosen Publishing, [2025] | Series: @RosenTeenTalk:
   life skills | Includes index.
Identifiers: LCCN 2024008039 (print) | LCCN 2024008040 (ebook) | ISBN
   9781499477511 (library binding) | ISBN 9781499477504 (paperback) | ISBN
   9781499477528 (ebook)
Subjects: LCSH: Vocational guidance--Juvenile literature. | Job
   hunting--Juvenile literature.
Classification: LCC HF5381.2 .K525 2025 (print) | LCC HF5381.2 (ebook) |
   DDC 331.702--dc23/eng/20240319
LC record available at https://lccn.loc.gov/2024008039
LC ebook record available at https://lccn.loc.gov/2024008040

Manufactured in the United States of America
CPSIA Compliance Information: Batch #CSRYA25. For Further Information contact Rosen Publishing at 1-800-237-9932.

Find us on

CONTENTS

Chapter 1

Gas Money

I'm so excited! I just got my learner's permit. I can't wait to learn to drive. My folks said if I want to use the car, I need to pay for gas. I also need to give them money for **insurance**. I guess I need a job.

There's a help wanted poster in the supermarket. I don't know if I want to spend my whole summer there. Maybe I'll look online. My **guidance counselor** can help me apply for working papers. Maybe they can tell me a good website for finding a job.

I think I'd like to be outside. Maybe the garden center is hiring. It'll be really cool to have my own money. But...I'm just not sure what kind of job I want.

> Getting your first job is an important first step toward independence.

STUDENT FIRST

If you're still in school, it's important to remember that you're a student first. That's your number-one focus. Even if you don't want to go to college right now, you need your high school diploma. It's required for most entry-level jobs. It's also needed for most **apprenticeship** programs.

High school students can apply for jobs. However, you need government-issued working papers. You need to attend school. Your working papers can be taken away for poor grades or skipping school.

A summer job really doesn't matter much in the long run. Your grades are more important to your future.

DID YOU KNOW?

Even kids who work in theater, movies, or on TV shows go to school. They have to keep their grades up or they won't be allowed to work.

WORKING PAPERS

If you're under 18 you need working papers to get a job. There are federal (national) and local laws about what kinds of jobs you can do. There are also rules about how many hours you can work. Working papers are issued by your local government. Your employer keeps them on file.

Your guidance counselor can give you an application, or form, for working papers. You'll need your **Social Security** number, birth **certificate**, and proof that you received a doctor's check-up.

What For?

Your Social Security number is proof of who you are for tax purposes.

Your birth certificate is proof that you're old enough to work.

The doctor's note is proof that you're healthy enough to work.

There are laws to keep working teens safe. They're set up to make sure kids have enough time to rest and do their schoolwork.

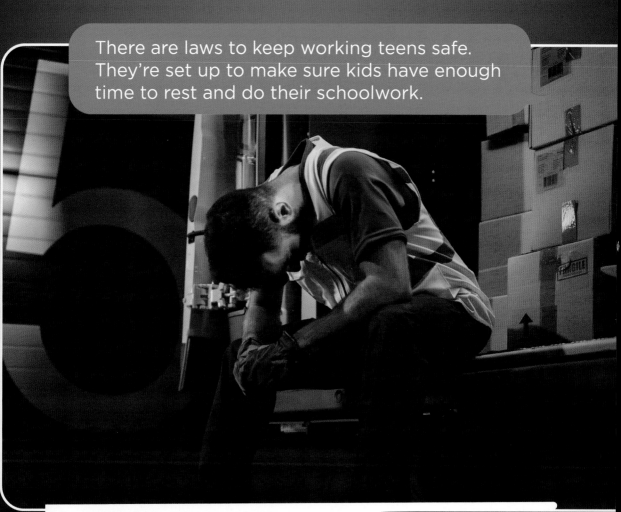

FINDING A JOB

Today, most jobs are posted online. Look at the websites for big chain stores like Walmart or CVS. If you scroll down to the bottom of the page, you'll see a link that says something like "careers" or "employment" or "work for us." This link will show you information about working for the store. It will include their hiring practices and applications. Some companies don't hire people younger than 18. Read the rules carefully before starting an application.

Online Job Search

Many companies post job listings on sites like Indeed.com. This is a trustworthy website that has good job-hunting tips. Always ask an adult you trust to check out a website before you enter any personal information.

Sometimes communities or school systems have summer job fairs for teens. Check them out!

LOCAL JOB SEARCH

Locally owned businesses sometimes post available jobs in their front window or on a community bulletin board. Many communities today have places online where you can find information about local jobs.

Chapter 2

WHAT DO YOU WANT TO DO?

When you get a job, you'll be at work for hours at a time. It's helpful if it's something you enjoy doing or in a place you like to be.

Would you like to work inside or outdoors? Do you have a favorite hobby? You might be able to get a job that includes an employee **discount**. Do you have a career in mind? Perhaps there's a summer job that can give you a taste of what that career is really like.

The "Perks"

Benefits (sometimes called perks) are forms of compensation, or rewards, in addition to a paycheck that you receive for working. Benefits can be things like insurance, retirement funds, or an employee discount.

Summer jobs at zoos can be fun! Keep in mind that most positions are outside. You will need to remember to wear sunscreen on sunny days. The attraction might close during stormy weather.

SUMMER JOB?

Places like zoos and amusement parks often have summer jobs for young people. They hire people to sell tickets and work at stands. Depending on your age and local safety rules, you might get a job running a ride.

WHAT SKILLS DO YOU HAVE?

When you're looking for a job, start by making a list of your skills. Are you a strong swimmer? Consider becoming **qualified** as a lifeguard. Do you enjoy being around younger kids? How about a job as a summer camp counselor?

What kind of computer skills do you have? Can you use all the programs in Microsoft Office? How about video or photography editing software? The more skills you have the more interesting jobs you can apply for. You may even get paid more for special skills.

If you enjoy swimming and being around water, becoming a lifeguard is a good choice. You can find jobs at parks, apartment complexes, gyms, or summer camps.

WHAT'S A RÉSUMÉ?

A résumé is a list of the places you worked, the dates you worked there, and the kind of work you did. No one expects students to have a long or fancy résumé. Basically, you want to share any experience that shows you're a **responsible** person they can trust.

Libraries have books about writing résumés. They might even have a free class or workshop.

What Are References?

Employers may ask you for references. These are kind words from people you know or work with. A professional reference is someone you've worked with before. They'll tell a new employer about your work habits. A personal reference is someone like a friend or neighbor. It's best if it's someone you've known for years.

REFERENCE

THIS IS ME!

What kinds of experiences should go on a résumé?

- work experience, if any (babysitting, mowing lawns, being a camp counselor, etc.)
- special skills (martial arts, computer programs, languages, etc.)
- clubs and activities (4-H, the Scouts, community baseball team, etc.)
  - this should include awards and honors
- volunteer activities (community clean-up project, soup kitchen, etc.)

Most résumés include education, but since you're still in high school, you may not have anything to say. You can list any education you've received outside of school (CPR classes, cooking lessons, guitar lessons, etc.).

Chapter 3

Beauty School

I've decided I want to go to beauty school when I **graduate**. My guidance counselor is helping me get information about schools and how to pay for them. I want to get a head start on my career this summer.

I want to get a job where I can learn about different beauty products and maybe even get a discount. I've made a list of places I want to apply to: the beauty supply superstore, the makeup counter at the department store, and the two big-box pharmacies.

I also want to check out all the salons in town. I want to ask people where they went to school. I'd also like to know if it's better to specialize or take a full **cosmetology** program.

If you have a career in mind, you might be able to start working toward that goal with your first job.

APPLYING FOR A JOB

The first step to being hired is filling out a job application. This will ask for your name, address, and contact information. It will ask if it's legal, or lawful, for you to work in the United States. It will also ask how you heard about the job and why you want to work for the company.

Today, most job applications are online. Before you fill anything out, have a trusted adult check the site to make sure it's safe.

one
r
or a
hey can
person to
ference.

B SEARCHING ONLINE

g websites are a good start when searching for local jobs

ndeed.com

jobs2careers.com

PREPARING FOR AN INTERVIEW

A job interview is a meeting with an employer you'd like to work for. If you're called for an interview, it means they liked your application and want to meet you in person. During the interview, they'll ask questions. They'll probably ask why you want to work for them.

You'll get to ask questions too. If you applied to a store, you might ask if you'll be working on the sales floor, in the stockroom, or at a cash register. You should practice some questions and answers with someone close to you.

A good interviewer wants you to be comfortable. They want to find out if you're a good choice for their job.

PREPARE TO BE PROFESSIONAL

Be careful how you answer the phone when you're applying for jobs. A simple "Hello, Lopez residence, Jason speaking" works well. If you use your own cell phone, be sure your voicemail message is clear and polite.

If you're applying for jobs online, consider having a separate account for job applications. "Your Name @ (free mail service)" is a good choice.

WHAT TO WEAR

Generally, employers don't expect a high school student to wear a suit to an interview. However, you should always be neat and well groomed. Don't wear jeans or sneakers. Choose a nice skirt or pair of pants. Wear a shirt or top with no writing on it.

The best thing to wear to a job interview is a friendly smile.

Your hair should be clean and combed. Your hands and nails should be clean. Don't wear a lot of jewelry or makeup. Definitely don't wear strong perfume or body spray.

Helpful Hint

If possible, visit the place you've applied to. See what the employees wear to work. That can give you a good idea of what to wear for your interview.

ONLINE RESOURCE

The Boys and Girls Clubs of America has lots of helpful information on its website, www.bgca.org. Use the search function to find tips for finding a job and preparing for an interview.

HOW TO ACT

You want to be friendly and polite to everyone you meet at the interview. This starts as soon as you step on the property. Don't rush for the last parking spot or let the door swing in someone's face. It could be the business owner or their best **client**!

During the interview, sit up straight. Pay attention to the person speaking to you. Don't chew gum. Speak clearly and don't use slang. Always thank the interviewer for their time and shake hands.

If the interviewer introduces themselves by their first name, it's OK to use it. If they say Mr. or Ms., use that. Sir or ma'am also works well.

You'll want to shake hands with the interviewer. Not a high five or fist bump like you'd do with a friend. Ask a trusted adult to help you practice greeting and shaking hands.

AFTER THE INTERVIEW

At the end of a job interview, the interviewer usually says something like, "We'll be in touch." If you've gotten far enough into the hiring process to be interviewed, you'll usually be notified of their decision.

If you don't get the job, be sure to thank the interviewer for interviewing you anyways. You may have another chance in the future.

You might be contacted by phone, email, or mail. If you've been emailing your interviewer, you might send them a brief note after the interview. Thank them for taking the time to talk with you and say you look forward to hearing from them.

If you do get the job, thank the interviewer and ask for details about when you can start. Congratulations!

Job Corps

Another kid from my school got in trouble during gym today. They kicked him out of school! I don't want that to happen to me. I want a good job and a future I can look forward to, but I can't afford college. What can I do?

My guidance counselor told me about something called Job Corps. They train kids like me for all sorts of jobs. She said it's free. I can live on campus and finish high school. I'd get meals and everything I need for my training.

I really like cars. In Job Corps I could learn auto mechanics. I could get the training to have a good union job.

Job Corps is a government program. It's free for qualified young people ages 16 to 24. You can learn more at www.jobcorps.gov.

Chapter 4

STARTING YOUR FIRST JOB

You want to make a good impression when you start a new job. Always try to arrive a few minutes early for your shift. You want to have time to put your things away before you start. Your boss expects you to be ready to work at your scheduled time, not after just running through the door.

Dress properly. If you have to wear a uniform, be sure it's clean. If you're allowed to wear jeans or sneakers, be sure they're clean and not ripped or beat up.

If you will be on your feet a lot at work, such as in a restaurant, a pair of tough black shoes with non-slip soles is a good **investment**.

LEARN THE ROPES

Your first shift at a new job might be an orientation. This means a supervisor, or the person in charge of you, shows you around the workplace. They explain your job. The information they share may include:

- company rules
- workplace behavior
- dress code or use of uniforms

- tax forms
- where and when you are allowed to take breaks
- employee benefits

PART OF A TEAM

Going to work is sort of like doing a group project in school. If everyone does their part, the job gets done. Everyone is happy.

If you want to be successful at your job, be a good team member. Arrive on time. Come back from your breaks when you're supposed to. Be friendly and helpful to your coworkers. Do all the parts of your job—even the things you may not like. Always keep your workstation neat and orderly.

If you're sick or have an emergency, always call your boss and explain the situation.

GETTING A BANK ACCOUNT

Once you have a job, you'll receive paychecks. This can be a good time to open your own bank account. Most large banks have special accounts for teens. Age requirements vary from one bank to another. If you're younger than 18, and definitely if you're younger than 16, your parents will have access to certain features of your account. Most bank accounts today come with a debit or ATM card that you can use instead of cash to buy things. You can also use a debit card to withdraw, or take out, cash from your account.

A "live check" is a paper check that must be cashed or put into a bank. Sometimes there's a waiting period of a couple of days before you have access to the full amount of the check.

Some big companies pay via paycheck cards. This is like a gift card that the company reloads each payday.

WHAT IS DIRECT DEPOSIT?

Many employers pay by direct deposit. This means your paycheck is deposited, or sent to, your bank account. The full amount of your check is available right away.

Chapter 5

FINDING A JOB THAT FITS

Having a job is a little like being in school. You have to be on time and you have to listen to your supervisor. There might be parts of the job you don't like—such as taking out the trash.

It's also different from school. There may not be other people your age to talk to. If you goof off, someone else has more work to do. If you're rude to customers, you can be fired. These things are all part of having a job.

It's important to remember that even though you have a job, it doesn't have to be your last job! If a job is not a good fit for you, search for one that is.

Your state's Department of Labor website has lots of information about what is or isn't OK in a workplace.

Any place you work will have a display like this. These posters list things like the current **minimum wage** for your area.

COMPLETE LABOR LAW POSTER

FEDERAL MINIMUM WAGE

EMPLOYEE RIGHTS UNDER THE FAIR LABOR STANDARDS ACT

FEDERAL MINIMUM WAGE $7.25 PER HOUR BEGINNING JULY 24, 2009

The law requires employers to display this poster where employees can readily see it.

OVERTIME PAY At least 1 ½ times your regular rate of pay for all hours worked over 40 in a workweek.

assessed civil money penalties for each willful or repeated violation of the minimum wage or overtime pay provisions of the law. Civil money penalties may also be assessed for violations of the FLSA's child labor provisions. Heightened

THINGS THAT AREN'T OK

Work should be a safe place. None of these behaviors are acceptable. Some are against the law.

- Using racial slurs (or any other kind)
- Making fun of someone wearing a symbol of their faith or culture
- Touching coworkers in an inappropriate way

If you see a customer or coworker doing these things, talk to your boss. If your boss is the one doing these things, ask a trusted adult for advice.

LEAVING A JOB

The right way to leave a job is to give two weeks' notice in writing. Even if you didn't like the job, you still want to leave on good terms. Remember, your next employer might be calling to confirm the dates of your employment.

If it's a summer job, your boss knows you'll be returning to school full time. If you've done a good job, they might ask you to work shorter hours during the school year. They might ask you to return next summer or during school vacations.

> If you enjoyed your job and feel you've done well, ask your boss if you can list them as a reference.

TWO WEEKS' NOTICE

Dear Ms. Jones:

I wanted to let you know that I'll be returning to school soon, so the last day I'll be available to work will be August 15. Thank you for giving me the chance to work in your store this summer.

Sincerely,

Jade Smith

PREPARING FOR YOUR NEXT JOB

When you leave a job, one of the first things you need to do is update your résumé and references. Your next job will call to confirm your work experience. Some companies will only confirm the dates you worked there. Others may give more details. It can be helpful to know the company **policy**.

Think about what you'd like to do next. Did you enjoy this job? Would you like to come back or do similar work for a different company? Or would you like to try something totally different?

> When you're working full time, you want to have a new job lined up before you leave the workplace. However, many high school students don't work during the school year.

I Got the Job!

I did it! I got a job at the garden center. Mostly
ing things out to people's cars. I'm pretty tired
nd of the day, but I get to be outside. The gard
er also does **landscaping**. Some of it's boring stu
nowing grass, but some of it's really cool. They
he contract to **design** flower beds outside the n
ping center. I think that sounds interesting. I'd
now how to get a job like that.

I get my first paycheck tomorrow! My dad is ta
o the bank to get my own account. He's also ca
nsurance company to put me on the policy. Th
going out to have another driving lesson.

I never thought I'd get a real job, but here I an

> Getting your first job can be a first
> step toward your future career.

GLOSSARY

apprenticeship: A period of time during which someone works for a business, often for no pay, in order to receive training.

certificate: A document that is proof of some fact.

client: A person who pays for the services of another person or business.

cosmetology: Beauty treatment of the skin, hair, and nails by a trained professional.

design: To create the plan for something.

discount: An amount of money taken off the regular price of something.

graduate: To successfully finish a course of study; to finish school.

guidance counselor: A person who gives help and advice to students about educational and personal decisions.

insurance: A contract by which someone guarantees for a fee to pay someone else for the value of property if it is lost or damaged, or to pay a specified amount for injury or death.

investment: Something that costs money but is a wise purchase.

landscape: To improve the natural beauty of a piece of land with plants and gardening.

minimum wage: The least amount of money a country or state says that companies must pay workers every hour.

policy: A set of rules that employers expect workers to follow, often supplied in writing.

qualified: Fit for a given purpose.

responsible: Being the one who must answer or account for something.

Social Security: A U.S. government program established in 1935 that workers pay into. People receive Social Security funds after a certain age.

INDEX